The State and
the Political Economy
of Reform in Syria

St Andrews Papers
on Contemporary Syria

SERIES EDITOR, RAYMOND HINNEBUSCH

Changing Regime Discourse and Reform in Syria
Aurora Sottimano and Kjetil Selvik

The State and the Political Economy of Reform in Syria
Raymond Hinnebusch and Søren Schmidt

Syria and the Euro-Mediterranean Relationship
Jörg Michael Dostal and Anja Zorob

Syria's Economy and the Transition Paradigm
Samer Abboud and Ferdinand Arslanian

The State and the Political Economy of Reform in Syria

Raymond Hinnebusch
Søren Schmidt

University of St Andrews Centre for Syrian Studies

Published by the University of St Andrews Centre for Syrian Studies
School of International Relations
Fife, Scotland
UK

Distributed throughout the world by
Lynne Rienner Publishers, Inc.
1800 30th Street
Boulder, CO 80301
USA
www.rienner.com

British Library Cataloguing-in-Publication Data.
A catalogue record for this book is available from the British Library.

Printed and bound in the United States of America

ISBN: 978-0-9559687-3-0

Contents

1
Debates on Syrian Political Economy Under the Ba'th

Raymond Hinnebusch

This volume addresses the role of the Ba'thist state in the political economy of Syria's development, with two contributions looking at different periods, using somewhat different conceptual lenses, hence with somewhat different assessments of the record. The first contribution by Raymond Hinnebusch uses the notion of populist authoritarianism to analyze Syria's trajectory from 1963 to 2000. The second by Søren Schmidt looks at the deleterious effect of patrimonial rule on Syria's attempted transition, under Bashar al-Asad, to a market economy. These contributions can, by way of introduction, be usefully located in the context of the evolving debates in the literature on Syrian political economy.

State and Revolution

An early debate was whether the Ba'th party launched a revolution as it claimed or a mere coup. In fact most appropriate is arguably Trimberger's (1978) concept of 'revolution from above.' Both Heydemann (1999) and Waldner (1999) view the political struggle after the coup as reflective of a wider and typical conflict between agrarian oligarchies and newly emergent social forces, hence a developmental watershed. For Heydemann the strength of Ba'thist authoritarianism was a function of the social class struggles out of which it emerged. Hinnebusch stressed the role of party and corporatist institutions in forging a middle class-peasant, urban-rural, cross-sectarian constituency around the regime, findings later confirmed by Batatu (1999). The revolution also unleashed rapid social mobility for plebeian strata, especially from the villages and minorities. These analysts also embraced the concept of 'Populist Authoritarianism (PA)' for understanding the regime which took shape--one that consolidated itself by breaking the dominance of the oligarchy and mobilizing popular sectors. To be sure, by the late seventies, revolutionary leveling had given way to the construction of new inequalities and the consolidation at the heart of the regime of a new privileged alliance between Alawi power brokers and the Damascene Sunni merchant class. This 'military-mercantilist complex' (in Sadiq al-Azm words) was a crucial factor in regime stabilization which accompanied the end of revolution from above.

Political Economy under Hafiz al-Asad

A major issue was the nature of the new political economy forged under the Ba'th. Perthes' definitive, *Political Economy of Syria* (1995), made a strong case that after Asad's consolidation of power, the regime came to serve the interests of a new 'state bourgeoisie.' In particular during the mid-1980s second period of economic liberalization—with its austerity, private sector revival and export promotion, but *not* privatization of the public sector—the lower and middle strata suffered income losses while a new rich emerged. Regime policy roughly reflected the interests of the dominant forces in the regime's coalition--the state bourgeoisie, crony capitalists, the commercial bourgeoisie and rich peasantry—checked only by the residual ability of the party bases and trade unions to defend the interests of the public sector and the broader peasant constituency of the regime.

Reform under Bashar

After his succession, Bashar al-Asad set out, Perthes (2004) argues, to 'modernize authoritarianism,' to make the system work better so that it could survive and deliver enough economic development to secure the economic base of the regime. This was made urgent by the combination of rising unemployment and the decline of the oil revenues on which state expenditures had long relied.

Sharply debated was how far Bashar stood for reform and if so, how much freedom he had to push change. Perthes found that he was able to establish himself as 'the prime decision maker' and that his reform team represented the dominant tendency in the regime. He also engineered, within three years of succession, a renovation of the political elite, with a turnover of 60% in top offices, thereby transferring power to a new generation. His priorities were reflected in those he recruited to ministerial office, most of whom could be characterized as technocrats with Western advanced degrees in economics and engineering and favoring integration into the world economy. By 2005, he had consolidated his power without resort to violence, purges or repression and largely through legal and institutional means.

Accounts by Lesch (2005) and Leverett (2005) largely agree that Ba'thist ideology no longer governed policy and liberalizing reform was a strategic choice. Bashar, lacking an elaborate blueprint to substitute for Ba'thism proceeded by trial and error so as to not to risk stability. Syria would pursue a middle way: bucking the neo-liberal trend in regard to crash privatization, the shrinking of the public sector would have to run parallel with growing of the private sector, not precede it; at the same time, however, joining the Euro-Med partnership would lower barriers to global integration and undermine vested interests obstructing a deepening of the market economy. The first priorities were to foster modernizing cadres and to strengthen state institutions through administrative reform. But bureaucratic, legal and political obstacles slowed down even this modest reform program, while corruption, crony capitalists and the lack of accountability remained a major disincentive to getting the investment that alone could make reform a success. And, the immediate consequence of capitalist reform was growing inequality. Signs of a post-populist turn could be seen in the emergence of new state-sponsored inequalities resulting from 'networks of privilege' forged between state elites and their private sector partners and the shaving of the subsidies on bread and fuel that had been part of the populist social contract; the emerging oligarchic capitalism meant less a competitive market than replacement of public with private monopolies (Haddad 1999).

Syria was not, Bashar believed, ready for imported Western style democracy, and certainly not when economic reform meant belt-tightening for the majority and enrichment for the new capitalists. Political change would eventually come about, but it would build upon social and economic modernization rather than precede it. Syria aspired to follow the East Asian model of economic modernization first, then democratization.

Søren Schmidt's paper in this volume argues that exactly because the regime has not created the institutions that allowed East Asian developers to benefit from the market, the move to the market is likely to generate a predatory crony capitalism. Such crony capitalism may, in the absence of rule of law and of state autonomy and capacity merely drive out productive investment, as Schmidt argues. Alternatively, his assessment may be too bleak or un-nuanced and a period of crony capitalism might be seen as a fairly normal stage in the transition from a statist to a market economy. Much will depend, as he argues, on state institutional development not falling too far behind the unleashing of market forces. In the meantime, however, Syria's populist authoritarianism appears to have made the decisive turn to a post-populist variant in which authoritarian power is put in the service of the new stratum of crony capitalists, increasing inequality rather than growth and welfare.

2
Syria Under the Ba'th: The Political Economy of Populist Authoritarianism[1]

Raymond Hinnebusch

Conceputalizing PA and the Syrian Case

Syria's Ba'th regime may best be understood as a version of the dominant form of state in the Middle East, the prototypes of which were the region's most successful and imitated state building experiments, Ataturk's Turkey and Nasser's Egypt. This regime type may best be labelled 'populist authoritarianism.' Populist authoritarian (PA) regimes embody a post-decolonization state-building strategy adopted by nationalist elites which face simultaneous external threat and internal instability. New entrants to the international system at the bottom of the world power hierarchy and on the 'periphery' of the world capitalist system, they also seek to consolidate independence through state led 'defensive modernisation' based on import substitute industrialisation in the virtual absence of an industrial bourgeoisie.

Revolution from above

These regimes, artefacts of the early stages of state building, led by new elites from the small middle class intelligentsia but also of lower-middle class or plebeian origin, and initially based primarily on command of the military and bureaucracy, face the challenge of winning legitimation for their power among the mass public. Their state building project is seen to require, in Trimberger's (1978) words, a 'revolution from above.' Such a revolution effects a major transformation in elites, political institutions and social structure but is initiated from above by 'reform coup' and without the mass violence and insurrection from below typical of great revolutions. The Ba'th case also has features of what Walton (1984) calls 'national revolts' from below, that is, social movements which have many of the ingredients of 'great revolutions,'

5

albeit less explosively combined. A radical coup grew out of an anti-oligarchy alliance of the rural lower middle class, including strategic elements of the officer corps, with marginalized minorities and a significant proportion of the peasantry mobilised by agrarian conflict.

A PA regime uses its concentrated power chiefly to attack the old dominant classes while seeking legitimacy through egalitarian ideology and the political incorporation of middle and lower strata. This 'authoritarianism of the left' must be distingusihed from the more common and traditional authoritarianism of the right which seeks to defend landed classes and or pursue a capitalist road to development by disciplining the workers and peasantry. But PA regimes neither necessarily remain popular or representative of popular interests; indeed they suffer from a built-in contradiction between their attempt to mobilize yet control popular participation. Whatever their limitations, however, such revolutions from above have been the main vehicles of socio-political change in the Arab world where both mass revolution from below and evolutionary democratic reform have been rare.

Regime Consolidation: from Radical Jacobism to Bonapartist Presidential Monarchy

How is authority in PA regimes created? In Ibn Khaldun's Middle East-specific paradigm a new state is founded by a movement from the periphery fired by a vision of radical change which seizes the 'city'--i.e., existing power centres. Modern theorists stress the need for institutionalization. For Huntington (1968: 140-47) the seizure and *concentration* of power at the centre must be followed by the *expansion* of power as revolutionary leaders create political organisations, notably an ideological party, to mobilize new participants whose activism expands the political energy at the regime's disposal. Finally, the consolidation of new power requires, according to Weber, that it be 'routinized' in stable institutions, but this may take two quite opposite forms. Power may be *diffused* through legal-rational institutions based on consent and the satisfaction of (largely economic) interests; alternatively, it may be routinized in personal patrimonial authority in which case state power capabilities actually *contract* (Weber 1964: 363--373).

The Syrian case largely replicates this 'life cycle:' an ideological movement from the periphery seized power by coup, repressed all opposition and carried out revolution from above against its enemies. But the regime could only consolidate power through patrimonialization, at the cost of its later contraction. This was because in its Jacobin first phase, the regime was wracked by intra-regime power struggles (1963-70) that could not be confined to party and state insitutions; rather, contentors in power struggles, even when turning on ideological issues, made use of *asabiya*--kinship and sectarian solidarity--and Alawis, by virtue of their disproportionate recruitment, were best positioned to succeed in this game. The centre was stabilised only when one faction finally won out and its leader, Hafiz al-Asad, established patrimonial authority. Although Asad forged a cross-sectarian coalition, at its core were loyal followers (jama'a) from his Alawi sect. This personal authority was then semi-institutionalised in an office--partly bureaucratic, partly patrimonial: a virtual 'Presidential Monarchy.' Asad's authority was consolidated through his control of reliable instruments of coercion, including the 'mukhabarat' (secret police), but above all the transformation of the military into a reliable regime pillar.

However, coercion can only concentrate, not expand power; the weak state captured by the Ba'th had so little power and urban centred opposition had such effective means of resistance that regime survival required power expansion, that is, bringing in new participants through regime institutions. If the military and secret police are the key apparatuses for the concentration and defence of power in PA regimes, the single or dominant party is the key to the mass incorporation on which power expansion depends. Huntington argues that the Leninist party, with its core of ideological militants and mass auxiliaries penetrating society, is uniquely capable of both concentrating power and expanding it (Huntington 1968: 334--343; 1974). This 'mobilised participation' is crucial for the consolidation of PA regimes, but it may also make a difference for policy outcomes as well: arguably, the more the seizure of power is preceded, accompanied, or followed by social conflict and political mobilisation, the more the ruling revolutionary party will incorporate true activism, and the more enduring its populist orientation will be as its constituents become a constraint on dilution of the radical ideology and egalitarian policies initially used to mobilize them (Huntington 1974; Huntington and Nelson 1976: 7--10; Nelson 1987; Skocpol 1979). In the Syrian case, the Ba'th came to power by coup, not mass mobilisation, but a prior decade of social crisis and anti-oligarchy party activism meant the coup was a delayed outcome of prior political mobilisation which the regime subsequently reactivated and incorporated through the party and its associated corporatist structures.

Weber argues that, as ideology inevitably declines, new regimes must consolidate power through provision of routined economic benefits and opportunities, in the first place to core followers but also to broader constituencies. PA regimes initially create popular constituencies through re-stratification, the demolition of old distributions of wealth and the state creation of new ones (Apter 1965: 123--133). The regime levels the dominant classes, the most independent social forces; control of the public sector and land reform allows it to redistribute resources and opportunity, and thereby foster upward mobility for its constituency, while making mass society state-dependent.

The consolidation of PA regimes in the Middle East cannot, however, be detached from war, war preparation and the state's position in the international system. In the Syrian case, the insecurity stimulated by the Arab-Israeli conflict, especially the defeat in 1967, legitimated the creation of an authoritarian national security state. On the other hand, the resources for this project partly derived from Syria's exploitation of Cold War rivalries which allowed it to access Soviet protection, arms and development aid. Moreover, the oil price explosion in the seventies and Syria's status as a 'front line state' with Israel allowed it to extract oil rent from regional donors. This transformed Syria into a partial or indirect rentier state, with some of its new rent deployed as patronage needed to satisfy the regime's constituencies once redistribution was exhausted. Thereafter a 'loyalty system' developed in which systemic corruption, smuggling, extortion in Lebanon etc., bought the loyalty of the inner core.

The patrimonialization of the regime centre, combined with the fluidization of the social structure and the new rentierism, with its 'loyalty system' permitted the consolidation of a *'Bonapartist' regime*-- one led by a dominant patrimonial leader who uses the bureaucratic and distributory command posts of the state to balance and arbitrate between levelled old and rising new social forces. As the regime's autonomy of society is thereby enhanced, its orientation alters: defence of state interests--its legitimacy, capabilities, and resource base--is put above responsiveness to the regime's initial popular constituents. Intra-regime politics becomes bureaucratic rivalry over jurisdictions, resources, and incremental policy change while in society class conflict is displaced by individual and group competition for access to state patronage.

The weakness of institutions means, particularly as ideology is exhausted, a contraction of the state's power to drive change. There are various ingredients in this decline. First, PA's built-in contradiction between the incorporation of new social forces and the authoritarian compulsion to control them eventually results in such low tolerance of activism that the regime forfeits the 'political energy' of its own followers; it also sacrifices the potential of party institutions to check the tendency of power elites to treat the state as their private patrimony. At the same time, to the very extent regime consolidation ends the class conflict with the old oligarchy, the regime loses the functional substitute for competitive politics which hitherto kept it to some extent responsive to its mass constituency. Moreover, as formerly radical elites, using power to get wealth, are embourgeoised, lose their radical ideological commitments and turn into a 'state bourgeoisie' they became receptive to the use of wealth by privileged groups to buy political influence at the expense of their plebeian constituency. Finally, as the state is patrimonialized, the power of the regime to get things done, in particular to drive social change from above, melts away. All these tendencies were particularly apparent in the late Hafiz period.

The descent into patrimonialization and embourgeoisment generates two consequences which result in a substantial alteration in state-society relations. First, it re-generates opposition in society which in the Middle East, including Syria, takes the form of political Islam. Islam becomes an ideology of protest--even rebellion--which goes well beyond resistance by the old oligarchy to populist reforms and spreads to the much wider groups frozen out of state patronage networks or damaged by state intrusions in the market, notably educated unemployed youth and the commercial petite bourgeoisie. At the same time, patrimonialization, in enervating the state's economic capabilities, forces an economic liberalisation which revitalises bourgeois factions not readily controlled by the state.

The PA regime may counter these threats to its power either by repression or by appeasing the opposition through limited liberalisation. Its precise strategy depends on the balance of threat and opportunity it faces: specifically, while economic liberalisation pushes the regime to appease the bourgeoisie through some parallel political liberalisation, Islamic rebellion deters it from any relaxation of control. In the Syrian case, the dimensions of the Islamic challenge precipitated massive repression which deadened political life; yet thereafter, the regime, having eradicated all opposition, was positioned to concede a modest political decompression which appeased the bourgeoisie and substituted for serious democratisation. But power was barely diffused and the bourgeoisie remained too weak, divided or state-dependent to check the state or demand further political liberalisation. However, the decline in the capabilities of a regime facing a more complex society shifted the state-society balance of power against it. Thus, a regime which once had the power to enforce revolution from above could now, at best, manage incremental policy change. This is the state apparatus that Bashar al-

Asad inherited; as he discovered, it was not 'fit for purpose' in implementing the liberalizing reforms he decreed.

Political Economy under PA: from Revolution to 'Neo-Mercantilism:'

The authoritarian-populist regime ostensibly aims to carry out a revolution from above and establish a strong state able to hold its own in the international arena. In the early phases of the Ba'th regime, class-shaped populist ideology animated plebeian elites who concentrated the power to impose major social reforms against vested interests. Nationalizations and land reform broke the power of the oligarchy and initiated a levelling social revolution. The outcome certainly qualifies as a revolution from above. But the aims of the revolution were only realised at significant cost and moreover, once redistributive reforms were carried out, a new routinized state-led economy had to be insitutionalized to substitute for the old semi feudal, semi-capitalist order.

PA regimes have claimed to follow a third way to economic development, neither capitalist or communist. By contrast, Marxist critics insisted that they followed a state capitalist strategy, substituting for and aiming to create a national capitalist class and engineer a transition from 'feudalism' to capitalism. Neo-liberal critics, on the other hand, believed PA regimes merely generated rent-seeking forces obstructing capitalist development.

Evidence can be adduced for both such contrary and possibly unintended *outcomes* of the PA strategy, but its *initial logic* is better captured by the concept of 'neo-mercantilism' (Apter 1965: 408-16). A neo-mercantilist state fosters economic development, not just as an end in itself, but as essential to the creation of *state power*. Neo-mercantilism is essentially a strategy of 'defensive modernisation' which aims to counter security threats while diluting the economic dependency which is believed to constrain an independent foreign policy in post-colonial states. As such, the economic logic of *capital* accumulation (maximised in the capitalist paradigm) is, under neo-mercantilism, subordinated to the political logic of *power* accumulation--that is, creating the bureaucratic instruments of power, winning support through patronage and populism, and acquiring military capabilities.

Yet, such regimes are not wholly inimical to either economic development or capitalist forces. Import-substitute industrialisation is seen as essential to create the economic base of national power and may be pursued with enough success to leave a permanent deepening of economic development, despite much sacrifice of short term economic rationality. Moreover, unlike communist states, PA states tolerate, even foster a state-dependent capitalist class; although they also constrain it and their re-distributive reforms retard private capital accumulation, the private sector persists as an alternative engine of development which may subsequently be reactivated. Thus, PA strategies are, indeed, a 'third way.'

PA has, however, built-in vulnerabilities which make it a necessarily transitional strategy which is gradually exhausted. Bureaucratic over-development, populist distribution, corruption and military spending generate a crisis of capital accumulation while the vulnerabilities of import-substitute industrialisation result in trade imbalances and debt. Continued neo-mercantilism depends on acquisition of rent, whether from oil or geopolitically motivated foreign aid. Periods of rent boom, however, only further the over-development of the state, making it more vulnerable to economic crisis in times of rent contraction (e.g. decline of oil prices). Inevitably, once the exhausted state can no longer drive growth or provide spoils, it must start to 'retreat' from its multiple economic functions.

Meanwhile, neo-mercantilism fosters a new bourgeoisie at the heart of the state while permitting politically-connected elements of the private bourgeoisie to thrive. As the state's resources are exhausted, the state bourgeoisie begins looking for investment outlets for its (often illicitly accumulated) capital through partnerships with private and even foreign capital. This generates scenarios for economic *infitah*: revival of the private sector and an opening to the world market. Economic liberalisation, in turn, fosters further détente, even a certain amalgamation, between the state elite and both the new state-dependent private bourgeoisie and the remnants of the old oligarchy, thereby altering the social base of the regime.

This has certain political consequences. It is accompanied by an opening of corporatist access to decision-makers for the bourgeoisie while, at the same time, corporatist structures are used to contain protest at the austerity and economic reforms which shrink popular welfare and labour rights. On the other hand, a full restoration of capitalism is obstructed under Middle East PA by the rent seeking behaviour of neo-patrimonial elites; by the preservation of enough popular rights to protect the regime's social base which deters investors; by the reluctance of the state elite to share power with the bourgeoisie, a historical enemy; and because of the discouragement of private investment by war or instability. In Syria's case, this was compounded by sectarian obstacles to the amalgamation of the state and private bourgeoisies and nationalist obstacles to the Westward foreign policy re-alignment required to elicit major foreign investment. In addition, since partial economic liberalisation often initially results in import booms and debt rather than much increased private investment, the state will be reluctant to wholly abandon its economic functions to the private market.

As a result, the seemingly strong authoritarian state is reduced to incrementalism, its policy caught between persisting statism and half-way economic liberalisation. Its policy autonomy is curbed by the contradictory interests (bureaucratic, bourgeois, popular) it needs to satisfy which, in turn, obstruct the reforms needed to reinvigorate state capabilities and the economy.

Outcomes: The Political-Economy of Etatist-Populist Development under the Ba'th

What has been the actual empirical outcome of etatist-populiast development under the Ba'th?

Agrarian Revolution from Above

The main test of a revolutionary regime which rose out of the village was arguably its ability to implement land reform, a notoriously difficult challenge which few regimes get right. The outcome of the Syrian Ba'th's efforts is a matter of some controversy. Some have insisted either that the chief beneficiaries were the rural middle landowners (Perthes 1995: 80-94) or that rural change was imposed on peasants by an unresponsive bureaucracy (Hannoyer 1985). While such side effects did distort the regime's attempted rural revolution, my evidence (Hinnebusch 1989) and case studies by Metral (1980, 1984) and Khalif (1981) show that land reform was implemented with only a temporary loss of production and that small and middle peasants benefited from substantial land re-distribution and state support. The primary political consequence was the incorporation of the peasantry into the regime, giving the PA state a rural middle peasant base, analogous to, but quite different from, the alliance with the landlord class typical of BA regimes.

Ba'thist Etatism and Import Substitute Industrialisation

The Ba'th development model enshrined the public sector as the 'leading' sector which would dominate strategic industry, energy, foreign trade and infrastructure. The state would lead the industrialisation of the country required to build an economic base of national power. In fact, by 1970, the public sector had become the core of the economy and the state development plan and investment budget were its main source of expansion: thus, gross fixed capital formation in the public sector grew from 170 million S.P. in 1963 to 1,262 million in 1976, while in the private sector it grew from 355 million to only 655.2 million (World Bank, 1980, v. 4, p. 48). The state regularly accounted for more than 60% of gross fixed capital formation. In 1984, public industry employed a third of the labour force in industry but produced 78% of gross industrial output (SAR 1989: 77, 170-71, 508).

A role was preserved for the private sector in trade, construction and light industry. In the 1970s, the public and private sectors each accounted for roughly half of NDP. However, anti-capitalist ideology and public sector competition peripherialized the private industrial sector, diverting its resources abroad or into tertiary or speculative activities and keeping it on a small scale: thus, 98% of the 40,000 or so private manufacturing enterprises employed less than 10 workers (World Bank, 1980, v.4: 54, 166). Nevertheless, some small private factories protected from foreign competition thrived in fields such as knitwear, shoes and food processing by importing modern machines and buying supplies from the public sector (Longuenesse 1978; 1979). Despite two waves of economic liberalisation in the 1970s, this structure remained essentially unchanged through the eighties for, although liberalisation allowed handfuls of capitalists to enrich themselves as agents of foreign firms or in construction, tourism, black-marketing and importing, they invested little in industrial enterprise (SAR 1989: 77, 170-171).

The public industrial sector was, however, afflicted with bureaucratisation and politicisation which deprived it of dynamism. Planning authorities could not impose a coherent plan against ministerial empire building and political patronage. Overcentralization allowed plant managers little operational authority to enhance efficiency. Low pay, political appointments and rapid turnover meant a lack of quality experienced managers. There was a scarcity of technical staff since once they acquired expertise and experience in public industry, they moved to the higher paying private sector. Workers were seen by managers as negligent, obsessed with personal benefits, and unwilling to cooperate in solving problems. They were unmotivated because low wages forced many to work second jobs and wages were tied to seniority, not skill or productivity. Because wages for skilled workers were higher in private industry, they tended to leave public industry, making it the refuge of the unskilled. Excess labour was also typical because of a state policy of maximising employment, the use of the public sector to provide political sinecures, or because of obsolete equipment.

Similar problems existed in matching output to markets: firm managers had little freedom to adjust to changing market conditions and export agencies were habituated to a bureaucratic rather than a merchandising orientation. Low export capacity meant bottle-necks in access to foreign exchange, spare parts and raw materials, and many plants operated at low capacity as obsolete, under-maintained equipment broke down.

The financial performance of public industry was weak. Firms' plans concentrated on the volume of production, not profitability. There was little control of costs, 'big gaps' in accounting, and hardly any cost-benefit analysis which could measure the efficiency of different operations or investments. Factories tried to simply mark up prices sufficiently over costs to give a 10% return on investment. But social policy often dictated otherwise: some industries such as fertiliser, textiles, and sugar often were directed to sell their product at prices near or below cost, resulting in low profits or losses. Apparent profitability in public manufacturing (whether as a percentage of sales or assets), hovered around the 4-7% range in the 1968-1975 period (World Bank v 4: 1980: 180-181).

The result was that industries were, at best, able to self-finance machinery replacement and some modest modernisation. But the surpluses of the public industrial sector were insufficient to finance major upgrading or building of new plants. Major investment had to be financed by external loans and aid or internal deficit financing. In short, the public sector failed to become an engine of capital extraction and accumulation which could drive industrialisation and substitute for private entrepreneurship.

The Limits of Public Resource Mobilisation

The central vulnerability of the Ba'thist political economy was that neither public sector accumulation or taxation produced sufficient resources to finance the state's many commitments. Taxation only accounted for about 25% of state revenues. Domestic resource mobilisation only covered about 2/3 of total public expenditures on government, defence and development into the eighties (World Bank 1980, v. 4: 48; Clawson, appendixes 4 & 5). Indeed, development plans always expected to substantially rely on external financing, especially as Arab oil money became available; thus, during the expansionary seventies, Syria's ambitious 4th Five Year Development Plan (1976-1980) actually only expected public sector surpluses to finance 54% of investment and of this much was to be provided by Syria's oil revenue rather than the profits of its industry (World Bank 1980, v.4: 101).

Underlying this vulnerability was Ba'thist Syria's inability to mobilize sufficient savings to support high rates of investment. In the sixties (1963-67) savings (11.4% of GNP) covered a larger proportion of investment (13.6% of GNP) than later but the regime could only mount relatively modest investment efforts. In the seventies and eighties when a big investment drive got underway, the gap between it and savings widened precipitously: between 1973 and 1986 savings covered barely one-half of investment (Hinnebusch 1995b: 310; World Bank 1980, v. 2: 18; SAR 1989: 480-81; SAR 1984: 564).

The consequent deficits in government operating and investment budgets were filled by a combination of aid or credit. Arab transfers made up a large proportion of total financing, growing from about 13% in the early Ba'th years to nearly a quarter of the total in the eighties. The remaining gap was filled by deficit financing or foreign borrowing. Deficit financing varied from an average 6.6% of the total government budget in 1966-1976 to a high of 22.5% in 1976 when Arab aid temporarily dipped (Hinnebusch 1995b: 309-10). External borrowing (e.g. from suppliers) also helped fill the gap. Overall, Clawson estimates that although Syria earned $25 billion in exports from 1977-88, (1989:14-17) balancing its trade deficit depended on receipt of some $20 billion in civilian aid ($14 billion of it grants) and $10 billion in worker's remittances.

The End of Economic Growth

For a substantial period, notably in the seventies, the Ba'th state enjoyed economic expansion. Overall economic growth rates were a respectable 3.7% per capita per year from 1965-1986, better than the 2.6% average for middle income LDCs. Indeed, until the eighties the growth rate was better than the pre-Ba'th era average of 4.6% (1953-63). Though the sixties were a period of structural instability, growth was nevertheless a respectable 5.5% of GDP yearly. In the seventies, oil money backing dual public and private engines of the economy drove an impressive economic expansion: real GNP grew 8.2% in 1970-1975 and 6.8% in

1977-1980. A wave of public sector import-substitute industrialisation was combined with a boom in private light industry and construction fuelled by state expenditures (World Bank 1980, v. 1: ix; Clawson 1989: Table 1; SAR 1989: 491; SAR 1991: 485).

However, this expansion had several flaws which sharply limited its sustainability and impact. First, a great deal of the massive public investment did not produce a sufficient corresponding expansion in production. Thus, in 1971-76, the Incremental Capital Output Ratio (ICOR) in public industry was 5.14 ($5.14 of investment capital for every $1 of new output) compared to 2.28 in the private sector. Overall investment efficiency in the economy steadily worsened in the eighties, slipping from an ICOR of 3 in 1971-1976 to 10 in the 1980s. This was due to poor management, to the long gestation of many large projects, notably big irrigation schemes, and to the numerous bottle-necks, power breakdowns, and foreign exchange scarcities which reduced the capacity of new plant (World Bank v 1: 63; Clawson 1989: 36).

Second, although several five year plans (1971-80) gave priority to investment in crash industrialisation or to consolidating earlier industrial investments (1981-85), statist development failed to create a self-sustaining industrial base. Industry was diversified, but the import of capital intensive turn-key plants and the failure to build a machinery industry meant intensified, not reduced dependence on and vulnerability to external market forces (Perthes 1995: 25-44). The industrialisation drive failed to structurally transform the economy (whether measured by the proportion of GNP contributed by industry or the labour force employed in it) which continued to be dominated by agriculture and trade in the nineties.

Third, Syria's over-dependence on external resources and credit or domestic deficit financing had costs and vulnerabilities. It fuelled inflation which damaged the purchasing power of the large segment of the population on fixed incomes--the regime's own constituents--while the chief beneficiaries were speculators and traders. Then, when oil prices--hence export revenues and aid received by Syria--dropped, especially dramatically in 1986, the vulnerability of this strategy was exposed. Various economic imbalances greatly worsened in the second half of the eighties. Balance of payments deficits reached around a billion dollars in 1987 and half that in 1988. A $4 billion civil debt and a $15 billion military debt to the USSR was accumulated. Repayment became a burden and Syria fell into arrears on interest payments. A foreign exchange crisis became chronic--e.g. at the end of 1986 there was only $144 million in the treasury or two weeks worth of imports (Perthes 1992b; Hinnebusch 1995b: 312).

The regime responded with austerity measures which initially deepened the crisis in the late eighties. The engines of growth shut down: the state budget, the major source of productive investment in the economy, was flat for years, but defence took up to 50% of it. State factories closed for lack of parts and materials and from power shortages, resulting in an industrial depression. In agriculture, a growing scarcity and cost of inputs squeezed peasant incomes. The plummeting value of the Syrian pound, commodity scarcities, and government spending resulted in inflation running from 50-100% at the end of the eighties.

All this resulted in the stagnation of GDP after two decades of significant growth; growth rates fell from 4.7% in 1980-83 to a negative 2.9% in 1983-87 (Hinnebusch 1995b: 311-312). Given rapid population growth of over 3% per year, this translated into a painful decline of 15% in per capita income. This, coming after a period of continual expansion, amounted to a crisis worse than that which contributed to the fall of the *ancien regime* (SAR 1989: 490-91; Perthes 1992b).

The Exhaustion of the Ba'thist Statism

The exhaustion of growth, far from being merely conjunctural, was built into the regime's state building and development strategy. Its economic policy was less a 'state capitalist' effort to maximise accumulation, than one which put economic development in the service of state building. Import substitute industrialisation, viewed as essential to national power had, in itself, built-in limits and in Syria it increased dependency on imported machinery, parts, and financing without developing a strong export sector, making trade deficits chronic. This was aggravated by the inefficiencies of the public sector, which, in turn, were a symptom of a more general sacrifice of economic rationality to the political logic of state building. Thus, the regime's initial redistributive 'inclusionary' strategy fostered consumption at the expense of accumulation. Asad's drive to build a maximum sized coalition required patronage rewards for a wide range of actors which dissipated resources. The state bureaucracy was used to create employment and the Ba'thist 'democratisation' of patronage widened the net of corruption from a few families to a larger portion of the population. On top of this, the Arab-Israeli conflict added another layer of 'overcommitment' by the state. It dictated the diversion of public resources which might otherwise have gone to economic development into a massive military machine. The creation of the instruments of power--party, army, bureaucracy, resulted in bureaucratic over development straining the state's economic base.

At the same time, the Ba'thist model discouraged alternative sources of development. Protection of the regime's populist constituency--co-operatized peasants, public sector workers--constrained private sector capital accumulation. Partly owing to the lack of business confidence, much private enterprise took the form of real estate speculation and import-export operations which widened consumption rather than commodity production. The on-going struggle with Israel, in depressing investor confidence, channelled private investment into short-term speculative ventures, and made Syria ineligible for foreign private investment on an serious scale. Syria's front-line status in the Arab-Israeli conflict did make it eligible for massive Arab aid but this, in relieving the regime of the urgency of choice between development and defence and easing pressures for economic reform, merely postponed a serious attack on the root of the problem.

The economic troubles of the late eighties did, however, put growing pressure on the state to alter its strategy. The fiscal crisis forced the regime into austerity measures which, in cutting populist welfare and investment expenditures, amounted to a certain withdrawal of the state from its core economic responsibilities; as the state withdrew, it encouraged a revival of the private sector to fill the gap. Moreover, as the state economy stagnated, a semi-illicit economy developed, based on the smuggling of commodities and foreign exchange and often financed by remittances of Syrians abroad. Austerity also generated a greater receptivity toward free enterprise among the Ba'th's constituents who, previously dependent on state patronage, now had to diversify their resources by setting up petty businesses. It was in these conditions that the regime began to move away from statism and toward economic liberalisation (Perthes 1991, 1992a).

The Politics of Selective Economic Liberalisation

Economic pressures did not mechanically dictate liberalisation but were mediated through a policy process in which contending interests sought to shape the outcome while the top political elite sought to contain the crisis and calibrate the extent of economic liberalisation according to the changing balance of costs, benefits, pressures and opportunities.

On the one hand, the extent, depth and rapidity of economic liberalisation were constrained by the interest of the regime and its core constituencies in maintaining a major role for the state in the economy. First, the power elite, recruited through a socialist party and a sect which used the state as a ladder of advancement, had a powerful stake in statism. This was reinforced by the corruption of elites who were enriched on smuggling or payoffs to evade bureaucratic regulations. Those who normally would bear the costs of liberalisation--public employees, workers--were part of the regime coalition while the beneficiaries--the bourgeoisie--was a historic rival on which the state could not afford to become excessively dependent. The regime's precarious legitimacy rested, in part, on providing welfare and economic opportunity for the popular strata in its original constituency and political logic required it protect its worker and peasant base from the encroachment of a revived bourgeoisie. In addition, the potentially dangerous urban mass, susceptible to bourgeois-backed Islamicism, had to be placated with cheap food and jobs. Moreover, the public sector had to be protected as the state's main revenue base; public sector surpluses, amounting to around 10% of total GDP, financed more than a third of all state expenditures and this could not readily be replaced by easily evaded taxes on the private sector (Hinnebusch 1995b: 309). Finally, the army's priority claims on economic resources as long as the conflict with Israel persisted, dictated continued state control over the economy.

On the other hand, variations in economic pressures and opportunities periodically altered the cost-benefit calculus of policy makers. After 1986, mounting resource scarcities seemed to give the regime no alternative to liberalisation; but the beginning of production in new high quality oil fields combined with a break in the bad weather for agriculture which plagued the country in the eighties, provided some relief from the tightening economic noose on the regime at the end of the decade. Syria's 1990 stand against Iraq in the Gulf war was rewarded with large payments from Saudi Arabia and the Gulf states which gave the regime further breathing room (Hinnebusch 1995b: 313). But shortly thereafter the collapse of Soviet and Eastern bloc markets removed any alternative to fuller integration into the world capitalist market. With the seemingly permanent stagnation of oil prices, further influxes of Arab Gulf money into Syria looked likely to take the form of private investments rather than state aid. At the same time, the state began to perceive opportunities from economic liberalisation: there was considerable hidden local capital as well as private capital accumulation held abroad by Syrians or by Syrian expatriates which, under more liberalised conditions, might be invested in productive enterprise in Syria.

However, economic liberalisation, to be economically effective and politically unthreatening, required the emergence of a reconstructed bourgeoisie on good terms with the regime and prepared to invest and to push for liberalisation. In the late eighties, the state-connected wings of the Syrian bourgeoisie saw opportunities to profit from selective liberalisation but wanted continued protection and a role for the state as a source of contracts and monopolies. Moreover, the bourgeoisie as a whole remained largely commercial and rent-seeking, its industrial wing weak and unable to substitute for the public sector (Bahout 1994; Perthes 1991, 1992a; Hinnebusch 1995b: 313-15; Hinnebusch 1997: 251-2).

The rough balance at the start of the nineties between rising forces for economic liberalisation and weakened but entrenched interests opposed to it, allowed the top elite some autonomy to shape economic policy according to its own changing ideologies and interests. Under Asad, the parameters of economic policy were always framed by raison d'etat: just as statism was partly a function of bipolarity and Soviet aid, and his early liberalisation measures, of the need to repair national unity in preparation for war, so the disappearance of Soviet power and the contraction of Soviet aid, technology and markets meant an international political economy hostile to etatism. Although Asad was unwilling to promote the complete unravelling of the statist system he had helped construct, selected economic liberalisation, in further co-opting the bourgeoisie, could enhance his autonomy of the party, army, and Alawi jama'a and hence his ability to accommodate Syria to post-Cold War globalization.

By 1990 an elite consensus had consolidated around the desirability of controlled economic liberalisation (Heydemann 1992). Once powerful socialist ideological resistance to liberalisation was dissipated by the embourgeoisment of the elite. Crucially, the climate shifted in favour of liberalisation as business partnerships developed between the private sector and the children of the political elite, who increasingly felt themselves, as their fathers never had, to be part of the bourgeoisie and who were confident that economic liberalisation would work for them. The exhaustion of the public sector and the collapse of communism put remaining party ideologues on the defensive. The ideological insistence on the public sector as the 'leading sector' increasingly gave way to acceptance of private investors as full permanent partners in development.

Nevertheless, there was also a pragmatic consensus that liberalisation had to be selective and carefully controlled. A Soviet-like collapse of the statist system before a market was in place had to be avoided. Because the private sector was believed to be mostly interested in short term, low risk, high profit enterprise, the public sector had to continue to invest in strategic industries. While the private sector would be encouraged to specialise in production for export, the public sector would continue to meet basic popular consumption needs. The public sector would not be privatised but it had to be reformed and made more profit driven (Sukkar 1994). This strategy, it was thought, would diversify the country's economic base, minimise risk and enable the top elite to continue balancing between the bourgeoisie and the regime's bureaucratic and plebeian constituencies.

Within these parameters, the extent and pace of liberalisation was determined in good part by bureaucratic politics: an intra-regime competition between liberalising 'technos' and statist 'politicos.' (Hinnebusch 1997; Perthes 1995: 203-271). The technos were relatively strengthened by the declining credibility of statism; moreover, in the 1990s Asad, pushed the party from its monopoly of policy making while giving business semi-institutionalised access to policy makers, further tilting the power balance toward liberalizers. The liberal wing of the elite was led by technocrat-ministers such as Muhammed al-Imadi, the Minister of Economy and Foreign Trade, the most consistent and effective advocate of greater liberalisation. Party apparatchiki and trade unionists defended state regulation of business and the public sector as essential to the 'social contract' in which mass political loyalty was contingent on a state guarantee of a minimum level of welfare. This was, however, no sharp cleavage: Imadi was no free market ideologue and, having been educated in 1960s development theory, affirmed the need for a state role in the economy. The party was not uniformly hostile to liberalisation and welcomed private sector investment as a source of jobs and foreign exchange.

Liberalisation came in two waves. In the late eighties, state constraints on the private sector were significantly reduced; notably as public sector import monopolies were dismantled, the private sector share of foreign trade widened rapidly. Joint public-private companies, most developed in tourism and agriculture, generated common interests between state and private elites; while the state retained a share of assets and some control in these companies, management was in private hands and the companies were exempt from state planning and regulation (Hopfinger 1990). According to a leading private businessman, this approach, avoiding the opposition of the trade-unions, was Syria's special road to privatisation.

The centrepiece of the second wave of liberalisation was the major new investment law, No. 10 of 1991, which welcomed foreign and private investment in industry, permitted repatriation of profits, waived import duties and taxes and allowed investors to import hard currency outside state channels. Highly progressive income tax rates were slashed (Poelling 1994; Hinnebusch 1995b, 1997).

These initiatives stimulated private sector expansion. In the early nineties--for the first time since the Ba'th took power--private investment significantly exceeded the state investment budget. By 1994, $1.78 billion had been invested in about 474 new firms under Law No. 10 and, by the end of the nineties, investment had reached $9.5 billion. A mini-boom pushed up real growth/year from 4.9% in 1987-89 to 8% over the 1990-94 period (Hinnebusch 1995b: 311, 317). The new private investment was probably not enough, however, to substitute for declining public industrial investment as it was largely confined to the tertiary sector; where private business did invest in industry, it was to set up consumer industries under European license, which could quickly recoup their investments (Perthes 1992a).

The investment climate was arguably not liberalised enough to attract sustained productive investment. Significant constraints remained built into the political system, including continued bureaucratic obstruction, corruption, and punitive currency laws which prevented many businesses from freely acquiring foreign currency needed for the imports on which their businesses depended. The relation of less favoured and smaller businesses to the Alawi barons still resembled the payment of mafia protection money. Private sector industrial growth took the form of a further proliferation of small enterprises owing to fear of government regulation, populist labour law and the absence of financial markets to finance expansion. Long awaited further reforms, notably a private banking sector and a stock market, were not forthcoming. Business confidence remained tempered by fear of post-Hafiz instability, lack of peace with Israel, and the weakness of rule of law.

By the late nineties, the Syrian economy was again stagnating, as trade deficits grew, drought devastated crops, and several international oil companies, unable to reach agreements with the government, departed. Significantly, Egypt, long far behind Syria in living standards, was riding a boom of investment which allowed it to nudge ahead of a still investor-unfriendly Syria in GNP/capita. Syrian negotiations to join the Euro-Mediterranean partnership suggested an awareness that sustained investment flows required further reforms. However, the increasing frailty of the president and the stalling of the peace process paralysed further innovations in economic policy, leaving the bourgeoisie increasingly frustrated as the new century was ushered in.

The Vulnerabilities Of Populist-Authoritarianism:
PA as a Transitional Formula?

Late developers like Syria may need a strong state to initiate national development and the pervasiveness of PA in the Middle East in the post-independence period suggests this was a dominant belief among state builders. But when state expansion exceeds certain limits, it becomes counter-productive. In Syria, the use of populism—what Waldner (1999) calls precocious Keysianism—combined with militarism, and patrimonialism to foster regime autonomy and capabilities overdeveloped the state relative to its economic base. The subordination of economic to political logic meant a crisis of public capital accumulation while the simultaneous diversion of public revenues into private hands fostered a new bourgeoisie in the shadow of the state. As such, authoritarian-populist regimes appear to foster the very conditions and forces which, over the longer term, undermine them and Ba'thi Syria was no exception.

PA regimes cannot wholly ignore the demands of economic rationality, and must, as statism reaches its limits, partly liberalise their economies and stimulate private sector revival. But political rationality deters the radical liberalisation which would jeopardise their statist/populist power base. The regime institutionalises power in social forces which, having established their dominance at the expense of the bourgeoisie, cannot look with equanimity on processes which would most empower this historic rival. Since populist authoritarianism, far from disciplining the masses, taught them they had social rights, full capitalist revival would arguably require a repressive exclusionary strategy which would alienate them and make the regime yet more dependent on the bourgeoisie. Ba'thist Syria exemplifies this dilemma.

In the nineties, however, Syrian policy makers still retained enough autonomy to balance social forces and shape a selective liberalisation compatible with the regime's social base and stability. Indeed, Syria seemed to be relatively immune to global pressures for liberalisation. The relative diversification of its economic bases--public and private investment, domestic petroleum and externally donated rent--meant that, while it had to seek a modus vivendi with the bourgeoisie, it retained substantial autonomy of it. It was also able to evade liberalising demands from international economic institutions (Perthes 1995: 6-7). And as long as Syria's regional arena remained one of conflict and insecurity, Syrian elites inevitably put undiminished state power ahead of economic development.

However as the state cannot continue to extract sufficient economic resources, it has little choice but to tolerate further economic liberalisation and as the state comes to depend more on private and foreign capitalist investment, it has to be more responsive to bourgeois demands. This is bound to have political consequences: it pushes toward a more overt alliance between the state and the bourgeoisie behind capitalist development, that is, a move toward the conservative bureaucratic authoritarianism (BA) arguably needed to begin rolling back the populist social contract which deters private investment. This is the route Egypt after Nasser has taken. Alternatively, the formation of a democratic coalition between liberal wings of the state elite and the bourgeoisie with surviving elements of civil society could push toward democratisation in which all strata would acquire greater freedom to fight for a equitable distribution of capitalism's burdens and benefits in the post-populist order. In the Syrian case, none of these alliances has matured but by Bashar al-Asad's second term all signs pointed to the former route.

In either case populist authoritarianism will be superseded. As such, the function of PA regimes may be thought of as mediating, for better or worse, the transition of Middle East states from their fragile underdeveloped starting points at independence to their reincorporation into the world system--perhaps now better equipped to hold their own-- in the age of globalization.

---

[1] This chapter is adapted from parts of chapters 1 and 6 in Raymond Hinnebusch, *Revolution from Above,* London: Routledge, 2001.

3
The Developmental Role of the State in the Middle East: Lessons from Syria

Søren Schmidt

Introduction

The role the state should play in economic development is one of the most keenly debated issues in the literature on development. During the immediate post-colonial period the intervention of the state was found to be important to solve so-called market failures which resulted in low-level economic development. During the 1980's the neo-liberals turned this wisdom on its head and claimed that corrupt and inefficient states constituted the problem of development and not its solution. In contrast to these approaches, institutional political economy underlines the crucial importance of the market in development as well as the need to supplement the market with institutions and in this respect stressed the role of the state. Institutional political economy does not see the state as being necessarily a class agent as Marxist state theory claimed, nor as a simple agent of redistribution, but as a provider of crucial public goods without which the market economy would not lead to dynamic growth. Or stated differently: without the intervention of the state, the private interests of market actors may not be aligned with the social interests of society.[1]

The objective of this article is to test a specific formulation of the overall thesis of institutional political economists that states do matter. I propose a hypothesis with particular relevance for the Middle East, i.e. that economic development may be explained by the structural variables of the capacity of the state and the role of rent in combination with the agency of state rulers. My analysis will start with a brief discussion of theories on state-market relationships and then quickly move on to discuss Syria as my case of investigation in relation to the three causal elements (state, rent and agency) relevant to my hypothesis. I shall then apply a more inductive methodology of enquiry and present six different contemporary case studies on state-economy relations in Syria. The case-studies are all contemporary cases of state-market interaction from the period 2000 – 2004 and represent significant and important issues pertaining to the economic development in Syria: investment climate, export promotion, liberalization of trade, financial intermediation and public economic goods. In the conclusion I shall attempt to use the analysis to discuss the present politico-economic situation in Syria with respect to economic reform.

Theories of Market-State Interaction

The market is characteristically composed of independent actors who freely make their decisions largely based on calculations of economic utility. You may give market actors incentives to do certain things, but you can't order them to do so (Przeworski 2003).

The state's role, however, is political. The state may characteristically order/compel and proscribe, for which it uses its means of centralized coercion (Stiglitz 1989). The actions of the state are not necessarily based on economic utility. Although they may be based on this, state rulers usually first and foremost look to their own incumbency or their own private economic utility as the highest priority, or to implementing a certain ideology. This is not predefined and must therefore be studied historically and empirically.

Are these two defining social ordering mechanisms of modern society mutually dependent? Or could we say, along with the neo-liberalists (e.g. Jagdish Bgagwati and Milton Friedman), that state-failure is the major problem and that the dynamics of the market are the benign forces of development? Economic history seems *not* to concur with that argument, as both late-industrializers (in Europe and Japan) and late-late industrializers (Third World countries) all needed the voluntaristic action of the state to overcome the low-level equilibrium they were locked into vis-à-vis economies that had already industrialized (Kohli 2004:8). This was the challenge that Russia, Prussia and Japan faced at the end of the 19th century (Gerschenkron 1966) and which all Third World agricultural economies faced at the dawn of the 20th century.

Economic theory explains this historical lesson by telling us that there are indeed a number of innate market failures beyond the ones identified by the neo-classical economists which lock developing economies into a low-level equilibrium of low productivity and low growth. Economic theory (Olson 1965, North 1991, Greenwald and

Stiglitz 1986, Bardhan 2001, Hoff and Stiglitz 2001) tells us that the market fails when:

- participants engage in fraudulent or anti-competitive behaviour
- transaction costs prevent markets from extending beyond restricted space and time and therefore prevent the economy from profiting from technology and economies of scale
- public goods, whether communication infrastructure, education, public health and dissemination or production of knowledge, are not provided.
- new more productive markets are not created, initial obstacles not overcome and network externalities are exploited

In all of these instances, there is a clear and positive role for the state to allow developing economies to exit low-level equilibrium traps. However, having identified what states should do to mitigate market failures, only raises the problem of another set of failures: the so-called state failures. Charles Tilly's theory of the classical triangular mechanism between military survival, taxation and an increasingly institutionalized relationship between the political executive and economic actors tells us that the state must promote economic development if it wants to survive (Tilly 1990). Indeed, such state promotion of economic development has taken place in most of the Middle East, but hardly as successfully as in Asia and elsewhere. While South Korea was a poorer country than Syria after the Second World War, it has in the meantime caught up and its per capita income was $15,074 in the year 2000 compared to Syria's $3,250.[2] Why?

The Capacity of the State to Project Public Power

When economic history and theory tell us that the state needs to intervene, intervene in a certain way and intervene in a non-partisan way as a public power, this immediately begs the question of whether the state has established itself as the highest authority within its territory, with a monopoly on the use of force and authority to enforce its rules and regulations. This cannot be taken for granted as the sovereignty of states is constantly being challenged by social forces and institutions. Before states can intervene in a meaningful way in economic life, they must by necessity first establish their internal sovereignty.

In the case of Syria, the historical process of state-building only started after the First World War, as it didn't exist as a state before it was carved out from the Ottoman Empire in 1920 by the French. So in fact, only from 1920 did the process start of establishing a system of political governance where the subjects of the state recognized the centralized and unmediated authority of the state (Anderson 1974). In 1970 – when this process had come to an end in Syria[3], authority was closely wedded to its coercive institution – the military – and the regime was propped up by a clientelistic constituency of peasants and state employees (Waldner 1999). These clients benefited in the short run from the established political economy, but the growing population outside this system did not. Although the state and the regime established their centralized political authority, they did this at the cost of a diminished ability to implement efficient and legitimate political rule. Public agency in Syria was not established on 'rational-legal' principles (Weber 1978), but had a neo-patrimonial character, where the minority Alawite military rulers established themselves above the Sunni majority community.

Although the Syrian state controlled the use of force and established its monopoly in this regard, it did not possess much power. Or expressed in the terms proposed by Michael Mann (1984), the state possessed a high degree of despotic power but very little infrastructural power, understood as a capacity to project concerted, social action by establishing a coherent and insulated organization that could regulate social and economic life throughout its realm.

The Role of Rent

Besides the historical struggle to establish the state and the political struggle for control of the state, an often-cited factor influencing the low capacity of states in the Middle East has been the prevalence of rent-taking[4], which constitutes the second factor that I propose in explaining economic development. The ability of the state to finance its activities without recourse to its societal constituency obviously diminishes the bond between state and society and makes the state much less receptive to what is needed to promote economic development and social welfare.

My point is not to establish a mechanistic relationship between oil and economic development[5], but rather to track the relationship between the weak state and oil-revenues. Strong states like Norway, the US, Great Britain and Denmark don't seem to be ailing as a result of having oil under their soil. But weak states do: in their case, oil exacerbates the defining feature of weak states, i.e. their inability to project infrastructural as opposed to despotic power.[6] Strong states have established an institutionalized relationship between the state and the market that promotes economic growth, but weak states haven't. Establishing such institutionalized deals is difficult and politically risky because they entail redistribution of political and economic resources in order to promote collective interests at the cost of special interests (North 1991). And when weak states get access to rent, they typically forgo undertaking such deals (Chaudhry 1997).

Whether directly as an oil-producer or as a recipient of remittances or of state-to-state aid from the Gulf rentier states, Syria may be characterized as a rentier state (Clawson 1989).[7]

Agency

While I propose state capacity and rent as the two structural determinants of economic development, the relationship between state rulers and classes, the outlook and ideology of state rulers and the inclinations and priorities of the supreme leader are all elements of agency which also play a role.

It obviously played a role that the Ba'th established itself in power in Syria as a populist-authoritarian regime and not as an alliance with industrial business interests as happened in South Korea or in Taiwan (Hinnebusch 2002). It certainly also mattered that the ideology of the Ba'th and of progressive Arab nationalists like Jamal Abdul Nasser were first and foremost redistributional and not economic-growth oriented as was the ideology of Park Chung Hee in South Korea (Kohli 2004). And it also played a role that Hafez al-Asad in Syria was a brilliant military officer, but had a rather narrow outlook and an almost all-absorbing interest in security matters (Perthes 1995). The kind of presidential absolute monarchy that he established in Syria as a substitute for an institutionalized political system, in combination with his personal inclinations and outlook, certainly played a role in explaining economic policies and how they were implemented in Syria.

Cases Studies of State-Market Relations

The following case studies are all contemporary cases from the period 2000 – 2004 of state-market interaction. The objective of the case studies is to probe into this relationship in order to extract some more general properties of this relationship in present day Syria. The cases represent significant and important issues pertaining to economic development in Syria: investment climate, export promotion, liberalization of trade, financial intermediation and public economic goods. It is therefore not unreasonable to expect that the findings of the cases will further qualify and strengthen the conclusions made so far.

Case 1: The Mobile Phone Company

Syria was one of the last countries to introduce mobile phone services. In the year 2000 the government licensed two private companies to supply the services: Syriatel and '94.'[8] Syriatel was owned by the Egyptian company Orascom (25 per cent) and by Rami Makhlouf (75 per cent), who happens to be the cousin of the Syrian President.[9] Orascom provided the management. The license with the government was a build-own-transfer (BOT) contract for fifteen years.[10] The other mobile phone company, '94,' was owned by the then Lebanese Minister of Communication, Mekati, and by Rami Makhlouf. There is no competition on prices, as these are set by the state agency, the Syrian Telecommunication Establishment. Competition between the two companies is restricted to marketing, customer service and signal coverage. The operation is hugely profitable.

In January 2002, Rami Makhlouf contended that he did not receive his proper share of the profits made by Syriatel. Rami Makhlouf's representatives controlled the cashier department and stopped paying suppliers to the company. The court in Damascus decided in March 2002 to impose a legal guardian (*haaris al qidaai*) and appointed Naader Kalai (a board member of Syriatel and representative of Makhlouf) as legal caretaker of the company until the dispute between the two owners was solved. The Syrian authorities then started to harass the Egyptian management: both the Egyptian CEO and the Egyptian marketing director received threats from the Syrian Mukhabaraat (Intelligence). Furthermore, the Lebanese lawyer for Orascom was not allowed to re-enter Syria. Finally, in April 2002 the CEO was given notice by the authorities to leave the country within three days. Orascom then filed a lawsuit in the UK against Rami Makhlouf since Orascom is registered in a UK dominion in the Bahamas. The case was recently settled by agreement on reparation payments to Orascom.

This case indicates that confiscatory activities are not only practiced by the state, but also exist in the private sector, where the state-connected parts of the private sector use their political connections for predatory self-enrichment. The most important institutional remedy to confiscation is effective and enforceable property rights. In this case the economic actor (Rami Makhlouf) was able to mobilize the public authorities for private ends and make a mockery of the property rights of

Orascom and, in the end, he was able to expropriate part of Orascom's property. The social costs of such selective property rights are considerable. They can scare away potential investors (foreign and Syrian) to the detriment of private-sector-based economic development. As Volker Perthes has remarked (2004a:38):

> 'If an Egyptian company with good knowledge of the intricacies of doing business in the Middle East was not able to prevail in the Syrian market, international investors are unlikely to be optimistic about their prospects.'

In addition to the convenience of Rami Makhlouf's father being the brother of the President's mother, he is also the head of the state-run Real Estate Bank. In addition, Makhlouf's uncle used to be the head of the Presidential Guard, whose sole objective is to protect the regime and whose leader therefore has considerable political leverage. Rami Makhlouf is in the process of expanding his business empire dramatically. The most spectacular of his activities is a chain of so-called duty-free shops at the borders, which in reality are shops that are not liable to customs and taxes like other shops selling imported goods. Rami Makhlouf's operations are all based on political 'arrangements' and indicate the degree to which predatory private interests influence decisions of state institutions.

Case 2: Grabbing Rent Havens

The 'Omar Sankar & Sons Company' is an old Damascene company that, since the middle of 2003, has been in a downward debt spiral.[11] The Sankar family is a well-known Damascene family belonging to the 'old' Sunni bourgeoisie. The office of the head of the Sankar family, Ihsan Sankar, is the headquarters for the only Daimler-Benz dealership in the country, but is also a 'public concerns' office that attracts envoys from around the country seeking advice or support. Ihsan Sankar, who was elected to Parliament in both 1991 and 1994, has for a number of years publicly aired critical views on the corrupt nature of the state-dependent commercial bourgeoisie, is an advocate of liberal politics and multi-partyism, and has set himself up as a representative of the old Damascene bourgeoisie.

Based on a trumped-up case of the company being in contract violation in relation to delivery of fire-fighting equipment to the Syrian Petroleum Company, a legal order was issued prohibiting the company from continuing the Daimler-Benz dealership. According to reliable sources, the person trying to take over the dealership is the above-mentioned Rami Makhlouf.

The case is an indication of the means and will of the regime to punish businessmen who dare to be critical of it and its associates. The punishment is the transfer of their rent-havens to politically more pliant businessmen. The case indicates once again how precarious property rights are in Syria and how easily they may be removed if businessmen cross the line for what is permissible political activity. The negative impact on the ability of businessmen to organize and play an independent political role, as well as the wider impact on market-based economic development is obvious.

Case 3: Exporters vs. Domestic Market Producers

Walid Suuf is one of a number of small textile and garment producers.[12] Suuf exports knitted fabrics made of mixtures of synthetic fibres and cotton to Jordan and Lebanon.[13] Thread is used as an input in the production process. As a measure to promote exports, tariff rates on input commodities for export production were reduced in May 2001 from 70 per cent to 1 per cent. Thread was classified as a production input and was consequently only charged the 1 per cent customs duty. The lower customs rate enabled Suuf and other exporters to buy better and cheaper thread, which in turn strengthened their competitiveness in export markets, both price- and quality-wise. The Syrian produced thread is supposedly sold at a price 40 per cent higher than thread bought on the international market.[14]

Textile and garment producers are small companies and not organized in a specific trade association. The companies are numerous and many of them are engaged in exports. In contrast, the two Syrian producers of thread are large companies and supply only the domestic market. The conflict of interest between the exporters of textiles and garments on the one hand and the Syrian thread producers on the other hand is evident. While the textile and garment exporters want access to cheap production inputs, Syrian suppliers of thread to the domestic market want protection from outside competition and consequently favor high tariff rates on inputs.

While Syrian textile and garment producers represent a dynamic sector with a huge growth potential, the same cannot be said of Syrian thread producers, who produce high-priced and low-quality goods for a limited and static domestic market, in which they can only compete due to protection from imports.[15] The economic and social case for supporting the textile and garment exporters rather than the Syrian thread producers seems evident.

However, when the owners of the two thread companies, who had good relations with Government circles, felt the cold winds of increased competition they petitioned the Government to move thread back into the high-custom category. This petition was immediately granted, without consulting the textile and garment producers. The end result was that the small advantage that the textile and garment industry had gained in export markets disappeared.

This case seems to indicate two different points. The first is the general difficulty of a large number of producers – textile and garment exporters – to organize and represent their interest vis-à-vis the Government. Mancur Olson formulated this as a general principle as follows: '...unless the number of individuals is quite small, or unless there is coercion or some other special device to make individuals act in their common interest, rational, self-interested individuals will not act to achieve their common or group interest' (Olson, 1965:2). It seems safe to add that in polities where self-organization is repressed, this inherent problem of large groups is exacerbated.

The second point to be derived from the case is that it indicates the existence of short-sighted rent-seeking coalitions between actors within the private sector and the Government (Krueger 1993) and the ability of these coalitions to thwart the Government's intentions to promote overall socially beneficial economic development – in this case by promoting exports.[16] The inability of the Syrian Government to implement an economic policy that is of general benefit rather than a policy of catering to the existing entitlements of economic actors clearly has negative developmental consequences.[17]

Case 4: Private Banks

In 2003, the Government finally permitted five private banks to start operating alongside the state-run Commercial Bank of Syria and three other smaller specialized state banks. At least fifty per cent of the equity of these banks came – as stipulated in Syrian law on private banks – from Syrian nationals, while the remainder comes from Lebanese or Saudi private banks. The Government also enacted a new law on the role of the Central Bank in overseeing these private banks and established a new board of Governors of the Central Bank with powers to fix interest rates and control exchange rates (Yazigi 2003).

On paper, such a reform seems revolutionary compared to the previous banking system, which mainly bankrolled the state sector and in which the banks operated more or less as general directorates under the ministries of Finance and Economy. Until June 2003 the state banks had applied the same interest rates for 22 years, whether this resulted in negative real interest rates (which was the case for fifteen years) or very high positive real interest rates (during the last 5 years when inflation was negligible). Bank services[18] for private companies and individuals were in the past provided by private Lebanese banks located in the Lebanese border town of Shtura, only an hour's drive from Damascus. Financial intermediation took place via semi-legal private lenders who did not have access to official adjudication and enforcement institutions. This resulted in short maturities and high interest rates because the high risks were discounted in the applied interest rate.

The lack of proper financial intermediation, which would allow for longer-term and large private industrial investments, seems to be at least one element in explaining why Investment Law No. 10 of 1991 mostly led to investment in commercial enterprises and light industries with low added-value transformation (Hopfinger and Böckler 1996).

How far can the new private banks be expected to address the previous lack of financial intermediation? First of all, these banks will not improve access to hard currency for investment purposes.[19] In Syria, hard currency is basically earned by the state from its export of oil, and the revenue from this export will continue to flow through the Commercial Bank to cover the hard currency deficit of the state sector. In 1999 the private sector had a foreign exchange deficit in its external trade of two billion USD, while the public sector (oil) had a surplus of USD 1.5 billion (Aita, 2002: plate 27). Should public foreign exchange earnings be redirected to the private sector, this would cause a collapse of the state industrial sector which the regime, for political reasons, does not dare dismantle.

Secondly, even if private domestic savings were provided for private investments, these would still be critically dependent on whether there actually were profitable investment opportunities. All the existing protected, private semi-monopolists have majority shares in the new banks and it remains to be seen whether these banks would in fact choose to finance any new ventures that would increase domestic competition and ultimately threaten these same semi-monopolists. In 2006 there is no indication that this kind of financing has taken place.

Thirdly, since the opening of private banks in 2003, they have received limited deposits, which indicates a problem of confidence. Is it realistic to expect that the Central Bank Board of Governors (consisting of representatives of ministries and three experts nominated by the Government) will have the courage to call in the equity capital of a private bank in case it defaults on its obligations toward its depositors? In answering this question, one should remember that at least one or even several of the hundred families that form a close alliance with the state elite own these new private banks.

Fourthly, the issue of the public industries is closely related to the issue of private banks and the role of the Commercial Bank.[20] If the private banks are allowed to determine their own interest rates, savers are expected to withdraw their deposits from the Commercial Bank because the Commercial Bank is not able to compete with private banks on a level playing field. The public industries are subsidized by 'loans' from the Commercial Bank, which however are very seldom paid back and therefore are de facto subsidies. Public industries are in consequence dependent on continued borrowing from the Commercial Bank and before the politically sensitive problem of the public industries is solved, interest rates can not be liberalized or determined by the market and therefore enable private banks effectively to act as financial intermediaries.[21]

Fifthly, how does the Government intend to improve the very limited technical capability of the Central Bank to monitor monetary and banking matters? In the absence of such monitoring and regulative capability there is a clear risk that private banks may be utilized as a conduit to extract foreign exchange from Syria to overseas safe havens through scams like those witnessed in Russia, Albania and other economies in the transition to market economies.[22]

Finally, it remains to be seen whether bank secrecy, on which Lebanese banks thrive (whether in relation to legal or illegal transactions), will be respected by the Syrian authorities, regardless of political expediency. The impact of the bank reform depends entirely on whether the relatively superficial and technical 'stroke-of-the-pen' (Page and Van Gelder, 2001) type reforms will be complemented by institutional and regulatory reforms.[23] The case indicates that the Syrian state is severely incapacitated in delivering such institutional and regulatory public goods.

The inability of the regime to go beyond launching a relatively superficial and technical reform and deal with the underlying institutional and political problems is clearly an impediment to realizing the economic gains from privatizing and liberalizing the financial sector.

Case 5: Free Trade Agreement with the European Union

In 2004 Syria and the EU (European Union) agreed to sign an Association Agreement within the EU-Mediterranean Partnership framework.[24] Besides clauses on political issues (convergence of positions, democracy and human rights) and security (anti-terrorism), the agreement stipulates the gradual implementation of a Free Trade Zone between Syria and the EU for industrial goods.[25] Free access for Syrian agricultural goods to the EU will be governed by a complicated quota system designed to minimize the harm to European agricultural producers.[26] Agricultural exports that exceed these quotas will be subject to standard tariffs for Most Favoured Nation partners which equal 6.5 per cent on average (European Commission 2003).

Syria already enjoys preferential status with the EU through the General System of Preferences scheme (GSP) by which the EU unilaterally gives tariff reductions to developing countries. However, the actual rate of utilization of the EU's GSP preferences by Syrian exporters is on an average only 30 per cent and varies from sector to sector. Even for types of manufactured products for which Syria is most competitive, the utilization rate is negligible. The utilization rate for 'clothing,' for example, is only 3.4 per cent, with 0.2 per cent for 'textiles' and 30 per cent for 'leather goods'. For the category of 'live plants, flowers, fruits and vegetables,' it is 60 per cent (European Commission 2003).

The limited use of GSP preferential access to the EU market suggests that tariff reductions are not sufficient to ensure the export competitiveness of Syrian industries. EU industries which have only limited access to the Syrian market under the present highly protective trade regime are in contrast ready for competition with Syrian industries[27] and it could be expected that, as a result of this competition, during the period of the implementation of the agreement, a substantial part of Syrian industrial production will cease.[28]

Trade liberalization is a hallmark of the orthodox 'Washington Consensus' approach to development. However, a number of studies have recently questioned the claim that there is necessarily a positive correlation between liberal trade regimes and economic growth.[29] The argument is that a liberal trade regime is only beneficial if companies are competitive and that, historically, the process of becoming competitive has always involved antecedent discretionary state intervention, whether in trade regimes, credit policy, subventions or other specific incentives.

This leads us to stress the importance of the state and its capacity to work hand-in-hand with private industries to develop industrial competitiveness. Without strengthening competitiveness, trade liberalization may instead be a recipe for deindustrialization. Rodney Wilson (1995:49) uses the expression 'second-rate modernization' for this development strategy, which he correctly characterizes as a process of retarding economic growth by replacing traditional crafts and occupations, which do provide added value, with menial production-line jobs, thus perpetually placing the economy at a comparative disadvantage to the West.

The Deputy Minister of Economy, George Habash, told me in an interview in 2003 that one of the motives of the Government was to use a signed Association Agreement as a political lever to implement new regulations which would be needed to make it beneficial for Syria. This view of the political objective of the Association Agreement is mirrored by Jerome Cassier, Deputy Head of the Delegation of the European Commission in Damascus, who in an interview with me (19.8.03) described the Association Agreement as a sort of 'antabus', which may hurt Syria and therefore perhaps 'force it to mend its ways'. In fact, Mr. Cassier agreed that it was difficult to explain the direct economic advantage of the Association Agreement. If in fact this is the 'real' objective of the Association Agreement, it is indeed a highly risky operation, as the likelihood of the needed changes being made and made in time is not known.

Instead of 'antabus', a cautious and gradual exposure to international competition combined with selective, temporary and cautious state subsidies to encourage and assist in the conversion of the Syrian industrial sector would seem not only to be sounder economically but also to be socially more acceptable and therefore generate necessary political support for such a transition.

Case 6: Delta Food's Export of Bio-Dynamic Tomato Paste

Delta Food is a Syrian agro-business involved in exports.[30] In the past, tomato farmers hardly used pesticides in cultivating tomatoes, and this allowed the company to export organic tomato paste to a growing market in Europe. After some years of exporting this product, the company experienced problems in ensuring the bio-dynamic quality of the tomatoes used for its production, as Syrian farmers also started to use pesticides. Although the company was willing to pay farmers a handsome bonus for bio-dynamic tomatoes, it has so far failed to secure a continuous supply of these types of tomatoes for its production.[31] The supply of bio-dynamic tomatoes requires that farmers are taught about the requirements of bio-dynamic cultivation and that production is supervised. A payment and contract system is also needed which penalizes production of sub-standard tomatoes and rewards the supply of tomatoes that comply with the standards.

Delta Food is a small company and the only company in Syria that produces bio-dynamic tomato paste. As a result, the company does not have the resources to provide farmers with the required instruction and supervision. Although the export of bio-dynamic tomato paste is a promising business, Delta Food is not by itself able to make sure that the costs involved in ensuring the bio-dynamic quality of tomatoes are commensurate with the gains that will accrue to the company. This is a classical externality problem, where the market is not able to internalize social benefits (Rodrik 2002). Externality problems must be solved by a third party delivering the required extension services and assisting in establishing a minimum size market, which will allow the costs of specialized extension services to be recuperated. The problem in Syria is that the utility of the Government Agricultural Extension services is very low, that the Ministry of Agriculture is not receptive to the problems of emerging export-oriented agro-businesses, and that there is not an efficient legal system which would allow companies to operate with contracts involving penalties and rewards in order to ensure the proper supply of bio-dynamic tomatoes. As a result, the potential of a promising business avenue, where Syria in principle has an advantage compared to other countries, has not been developed because of the absence of an adequate institutional framework and proper intervention by the state.

The Case Studies: Conclusions

The first case study – the case on the mobile phone company – indicated the negative effects of lack of separation between the private and the public realm as evidenced by the capture of state power by private individuals, making a mockery of property rights. This phenomenon may be characterized as neo-patrimonialism, where the ruler (and his family, friends and clients) prey on society and appropriate its resources, but do not try to increase these resources by promoting economic development.

The second case study on the Daimler-Benz dealership confirms the impression of widespread attempts of regime-connected private sector actors to confiscate other private sector actors' rent havens. Property rights, whether for rent-seeking or for production-oriented businessmen, are obviously insecure in Syria.

The third case study, on the customs duties on thread, indicates the influence of rent-seeking groups blocking the state from pursuing developmental policies. The Syrian state may be 'strong' and 'autonomous' when controlling the broader Syrian population, but in relation to specific elite groups, the opposite seems to be the case. This particular nexus between state and society seriously limits the state's developmental capacity.

The fourth case study, on private banks, underlines that if private institutions of financial intermediation are to promote economic growth they must be under-girded by efficient public institutions that, in turn, are based on hard political choices. As long as private banks are considered mere technical devices, they will at best not contribute to breaking the short-term and rent-seeking behaviour of economic actors and at worst facilitate financial fraud.

The case study of the EU-Syria Free Trade Agreement indicates that a macro-economic reform such as a liberal free-trade regime will forfeit its developmental objective if it is not underpinned by micro-economic institutions and policies which are able to raise the competitiveness of the private sector and that this depends on the initiatives and actions of the state.

Finally, the case study of organic tomato paste illustrates what happens when the state fails to complement the market by supplying public goods which are crucial for the development of a productive market economy.

Two salient findings emerge from these case studies. First, that economic networks between private-sector actors and public officials pursuing self-interests are prevalent whether these networks work to undermine property rights, establish rent-havens, transfer rent havens from one economic agent to another or prevent new economic policies. These economic networks seem to be a crucial mechanism in transforming poor state capabilities into negative economic outcomes.

The other finding emerging from the case studies is that policy reform measures did not encompass institutional reform and that this also seems crucial in explaining the effect of policies on economic outcomes.

Conclusion

The brief account of historical development in Syria lend credence to my claim that economic development in the Middle East may indeed largely be explained by the role of the state and rent and the agency of state rulers. The analysis furthermore provides evidence of the usefulness of explaining economic development not as an isolated economic matter, but as closely related to the process of state-building, which in turn should be understood as a result of historical political struggles. Socially desirable economic factors like capital accumulation, technology and education are in this view not causes of growth; they *are* growth. How these factors come about is what needs to be explained, and incentives provided by the institutional framework constitute a crucial part of this explanation.

Institutions matter in the sense that if a developing country does not get its institutions right, it is not likely to experience a lasting increase in productive capacity. With the potential to project and implement collective action the state is the most crucial institution in this regard.

The six case studies of state-economy relations gave evidence of the salient importance of the state in making the market economy work: Without secure and predictable property rights long-term productive investments will not take place. Without a state that gives priority to collective instead of particularistic interests, capitalism will not become developmental, but remain a limited zero-sum game. Without the state being able and willing to make hard political choices, technical institutional reforms will not deliver economic development. Without supportive and productivity-enhancing state intervention, free trade regimes will merely allow allocative instead of dynamic efficiency. Such a policy mainly benefits a strongly 'developed' economic party rather than a 'developing' economy, which is then left with the development option of trying to outperform other global competitors by lowering labor costs. Such a strategy is typical of weak states – like Syria – that pursue economic liberalization. The strategy is in fact 'a race to the bottom' because a first round of lowering of labor costs inevitably leads to a second round of lowering costs when competitors have caught up. Combined with the inherent inequities of liberal economies, such a development strategy will never gain broad legitimacy and will tend to discourage opposition parties from advocating market economy development.

The incumbent President of Syria, Bashar al Asad, seems to have had genuine intentions of political as well as economic reforms as evidenced in recent interviews (Lesch 2005 and Leverett 2005). However, the development of events related to the short-lived 'Damascus Spring' also indicate that the combination of the lack of political institutions, which could facilitate a new contract between regime and society and ultimately benefit all parties, and the fact that the president is beholden to a small regime-insider group with very narrow interests, played an important part in bringing these reforms to an early halt. While Bashar al-Asad might very well have had the intention to reach out to a broader political constituency which could have given him a freer hand in relation to the old power elite and allowed him to negotiate and implement a broader reform programme, the historical legacy of state-building in Syria made it difficult for him to renegotiate his political coalition/strategy in a controlled process and when the initiation of the political reforms quickly resulted in a regime-threatening political mobilization, these reforms were shelved and the old repressive system reinstated.

Syrian economic reforms have not moved beyond relatively superficial, 'stroke-of-the-pen' type reforms, either because the state was not able to undertake more complex institutional reforms or because special interests had now become so dominant within the regime and the President so beholden to them.

The result is that the economy has not been able to capitalize on liberalization of trade or banking or the shift from public to private production, and instead of producing growth, economic liberalization resulted in a zero-growth, un-dynamic, rent-seeking and and inequitable economy, which is more dependent on oil-revenue than ever.

---

[1] See e.g. Evans 1995, Przeworski 2003, Bardhan 2001, Kohli 2004.

[2] Both figures are in current PPP $, as are all per capita figures in this article.

[3] Military coups involving sectarian or regional interest groups took place in 1949 (3 times during that year), 1954 and 1955. After the Ba'th took over power in 1963, the army had to repress major anti-regime urban disturbances in 1963, 1964, 1965 and 1967 (Hinnebusch 2002:85).

[4] Defined as unearned revenue.

[5] As in Luciani 1990.

[6] For a full theoretical argument along these lines, see Karl (1997).

[7] In the early 2000s, oil revenues made up roughly 75 per cent of Syria's foreign exchange revenues, 50 per cent of state revenues and 30 per cent of GNP, *World Development Indicators.*

[8] The following is based on personal and confidential interviews in Damascus, December 2003.

[9] Makhlouf controls a vast business empire including Schindler elevators, Western Union money transfer, Shoufat International School and duty-free shops. The latest of his businesses is a shopping arcade being built on state land

next to the historical Hijaz railway station which is leased from the state for 99 years.

[10] Mobile phone services are natural monopolies or oligopolies, as they are associated with high fixed costs, which mean that services will not be offered if market entry is unrestricted. The ability to restrict rent opportunities in such markets depends, of course, on the ability of the Government to auction off, regulate and monitor such mono- or oligopolies. It does not require much imagination to understand that the restricted mobile phone market in Syria lends itself to huge rent-seeking opportunities, given non-transparent auction procedures and the degree to which the bureaucracy is penetrated by private interests.

[11] The information on this case study is based on interviews with diplomatic staff in Damascus in December 2003 and the article 'What Happened with the Mercedes Dealership?' *al-Iqtisadiyya, 30 December 2001:8.*

[12] Based on interviews with representatives of the company in December 2003. Names have been changed.

[13] Lack of proper transport facilities for export often makes it necessary to transport export commodities with travelers in suitcases. The advantage of this primitive transportation is also that it involves less trouble in getting the commodities through the customs (information by Walid Suuf, interview 2003).

[14] Interview with Manar Jallad, Damascus 7 April 1999. Quoted from Haddad, 2002:169.

[15] Textiles are a protected commodity in Syria. The main textile product produced in Syria is knitted fabric textiles and import of such textiles is forbidden. In contrast, woven textiles, which are only produced to a limited degree in Syria, may be imported subject to import duties.

[16] This is so even when it has been recognized at the highest level in Government that the main problem of the Syrian economy is that it has not developed a capacity to export manufactures (interview with Muhammad al-Imadi, 2003).

[17] Robert Wade (1990:129-133) provides an interesting contrasting example from Taiwan where a system of compensation to 'downstream producers' for the cost of Government protection of 'upstream producers' was developed.

[18] Like letter-of-credit and foreign exchange transactions.

[19] Although Mr. George Al Ouzone, member of the Managing Board of the Central Bank, told me in an interview in 2003 that this is the explicit objective of permitting private banks in Syria.

[20] Public industries are notorious loss-making operations. Stephen O'Dowd, economic officer at the American Embassy in Damascus, illustrated this with the example of the state-run refrigerator factory, which already has 16,000 refrigerators in stock and is still producing new ones. Refrigerators produced by a privately owned factory supposedly cost more than 20% more than refrigerators from the state industry, but customers still prefer these refrigerators to those from the state industry (Interview 12.1.04).

[21] I owe this point to Paolo Zacchia, World Bank Representative in Syria. Interview 20.1.04.

[22] I interviewed Mr. Adib Mayaleh of the University of Damascus in August 2003. Mr. Mayaleh said at that time 'I am afraid that the new private

banks may be used to take money out of the country and the likelihood that they will bring money into the country is low.' Mr. Mayaleh became the Syrian Central Bank Governor in 2005.

[23] As evidence of the naïve and technocratic thinking of the Syrian Government, Bashar al Asad explained to David Lesch (2005:215) that the main problem with banking in Syria is that they did not have private banking for forty years and that this time lag in learning is the real challenge for developing a private banking system.

[24] However, at the time of writing (May 2006), the agreement had still not been approved by the EU Council of Ministers because of disagreement between the two partners on Syria's engagement in Lebanon.

[25] The basic idea of the Association Agreement is to have any non-tariff protection for industrial products transferred into tariffs and then dismantled gradually over a period of 12 years. Interview with Jerome Cassier, Deputy Head of the Delegation of the European Commission, 19.8.03.

[26] The quotas are subject to variations during the year and may be changed or rescinded by the EU depending on the production situation of European producers. Such a quota system is hardly the best incentive for long-term investments in the private agricultural sector in Syria.

[27] Although Ghassan Habash, deputy minister of economy, in an interview with me maintained that imports from the EU are not in competition with Syria products because EU products are high quality, while Syrian products are not. However, Habash seems to take into account neither the competition from the newer EU members in this regard nor the fact that Syria needs to move up into higher category product lines in order to take advantage of the higher profit margins within these markets (see Evans 1995 for an argumentation along the same lines).

[28] During the period of restructuring of the Tunisian economy, it has been estimated that only 15 per cent of private firms will certainly survive the dismantling of import barriers, 70 per cent will come under serious threat, and the remainder will go bankrupt (Mahroug 1996: 91). The Tunisian industry is more competitive than the Syrian industry, so the Syrian figures would probably be worse. The Delegation of the European Commission likewise informed the author that approximately 2/3 of small and medium industries in Portugal closed down as a result of accession to the EU. However, at the same time, a number of new Portuguese industries owe their existence to the accession and, overall, Portugal has, he insisted, gained greatly from its membership.

[29] One example of such studies is in Rodriguez and Rodrik 1999.

[30] Delta's sole owner is a Mr. Rabaath, who illustrates that the problem of the Syrian economy is not a lack of businessmen with a good knowledge of the world of today. Mr. Rabaath has other companies in agro-industry in other countries and divides his time between Paris, Aleppo, Damascus and Beirut. The information for this case is based on an interview with representatives of the company in January 2004.

[31] Delta only buys tomatoes from farmers outside the cooperatives. Delta claims that tomatoes from the cooperative sector are of inferior quality, because – as the Delta representatives explain it – cooperatives don't care about quality as this does not affect the price they get from the Government establishment which buys their tomatoes and to whom the cooperatives must sell.

References

Aita, Samir. (2002), 'Euro vs. US$. Private Sector vs. Public Sector. The Syrian Experience.' Mediterranean Dialogue Program. Casablanca, July 12-13.

Anderson, Perry. (1974), *Lineages of the Absolute State.* London:Verso.

Apter, David. (1965), *The Politics of Modernization.* Chicago: University of Chicago Press.

Bahout, Joseph. (1994), 'The Syrian Business Community, its Politics and Prospects,' in Eberhard Kienle, *Contemporary Syria: Liberalisation between Cold War and Cold Peace*, London: British Academic Press.

Bardhan, Pranab. (2001), 'Distributive Conflicts, Collective Action, and Institutional Economics' in Gerald M. Meier and Joseph E. Stiglitz (eds.) *Frontiers of Development Economics,* Oxford University Press.

Batatu, Hanna. (1999), *Syria's Peasantry, the Descendants of its lesser rural Notables and their Politics*, Princeton, Princeton University Press.

Chaudhry, Kiren Aziz. (1997), *The Price of Wealth: Economies and Institutions in the Middle East.* Ithaca, NY: Cornell University Press.

Clawson, Patrick. (1989), *Unaffordable Ambitions: Syria's Military Buildup and Economic Crisis*, Washington, D.C.: Washington Institute for Near East Policy.

Evans, Peter B. (1995), Embedded Autonomy: States and Industrial Transformation, Princeton, NJ: Princeton University Press.

Gerschenkron, Alexander. (1966), *Economic Backwardness in Historical Perspective,* Cambridge Mass.: Harvard University Press.

Greenwald B. and J.E. Stiglitz. (1986), 'Externalities in Economics with Imperfect Information and Incomplete Markets.' *Quarterly Journal of Economics*, May.

Haddad, Bassam (1999) 'Change and Stasis in Syria: one step forward...' *Middle East Report,* 29/4, no. 213, Winter (1999).

Hannoyer, Jean. (1985) 'Grands projects hydrauliques en Syrie: La tentation Orientale,' *Maghreb-Machrek*, no. 109, July-August, pp. 24-42.

Heydemann, Steven (1999) *Authoritarianism in Syria: Institutions and Social Conflict,* Ithaca & London: Cornell University Press.

Hinnebusch, Raymond. (1989), Peasant and Bureaucracy in Ba'thist Syria: The Political Economy of Rural Development. Boulder, CO: Westview Press.

----. (1990), Authoritarian Power and State Formation in Ba'thist Syria: Army, Party and *Peasant*. Boulder CO: Westview Press.

---- . (1995b), 'The Political Economy of Economic Liberalisation in Syria,' *International Journal of Middle East Studies*, v. 27, pp. 305-320.

----. (1997) 'Syria: the politics of economic liberalisation,' *Third World Quarterly*, v. 18, n. 2, pp. 249-265.

----. (2001), *Syria: Revolution from above,* Routledge, London

Hoff, Karla and Joseph Stiglitz (2001), 'Modern Economic Theory and Development.' in Gerald M. Meier and Joseph E. Stiglitz (eds.) *Frontiers of Development Economics,* Oxford University Press.

Hopfinger, Hans. (1990), 'Capitalist Agrobusiness in Syria's Socialist Economy,' paper given to Middle East Studies Association Conference

Hopfinger, Hans and Marc Boeckler (1996), 'Step by Step to and Open Economic System: Syria Sets Course for Liberalization.' *British Journal of Middle Eastern Studies,* 23(2):183-202.

Huntington, Samuel P. (1968), *Political Order in Changing Societies.* New Haven: Yale University Press.

----. (1974) 'Social and Institutional Dynamics of One-Party Systems,'' in Louis J. Cantori, *Comparative Political Systems,* Boston: Holbrook Press, pp. 323--370.

Huntington, Samuel and Nelson, Joan. (1976) *No Easy Choice: Political Participation in Developing Countries,* Cambridge Mass.: Harvard University Press.

Karl, Terry Lynn (1997), *The Paradox of Plenty: Oil Booms and Petro-States,* Berkeley: University of California Press.

Kohli, Atul (2004), *State-directed Industrialization,* Cambridge UK: Cambridge University Press

Krueger, Anne O. (1993), *Political Economy of Policy Reform in Developing Countries,* Cambridge, Mass.: The MIT Press.

Khalaf, Sulayman Najm. (1981) 'Family, Village and the Political Party: Articulation of Social Change in Contemporary Rural Syria,'' Ph.D. Dissertation, University of California, L.A.

Lesch, David, (2005), *The New Lion of Damascus: Bashar al-Asad and Modern Syria,* New Haven: Yale University Press.

Leverett, Flynt, (2005), *Inheriting Syria: Bashar's Trial by Fire,* Washington, DC.: Brookings Institute Press.

Longuenesse, Elizabeth. (1978) 'La classe ouvriere au Proche Orient: La Syrie,'' *Pensee,* n. 197, February, pp. 120-32.

----. (1979) 'The Class Nature of the State in Syria,'' *MERIP Reports,* v. 9, n. 4. pp. 3-11.

Luciani, Giacomo (1990), 'Allocative vs. Production States: A Theoretical Framework' in Luciani, G. (ed.) *The Arab State,* Berkeley: University of California Press.

Mann, Michael. (1984), 'The Autonomous Power of the State,' *Archives Europeennes de Sociologie,* tome XXV, numero 2.

Metral, Francoise. (1984), 'State and Peasants in Syria: A Local View of a Government Irrigation Project,'' *Peasant Studies,* v. 11, no. 2, pp. 69--89.

North, Douglass C. (1991), *Institutions, Institutional Change and Economic Performance.* Cambridge University Press.

Olson, Mancur. (1965), *The Logic of Collective Action: Public Goods and the Theory of Groups.* Cambridge, Mass.: Harvard University Press.

Page, John and Linda Van Gelder (2001), 'Missing Links: Institutional Capability, Policy Reform, and Growth in the Middle East and North Africa' in H. Hakimian & Z. Moshaver (eds.) *The State and Global Change.* Surrey: Curzon Press

Perthes, Volker. (1991) 'The Bourgeoisie and the Ba'th,' *Middle East Report,* v. 21, n. 170, May-June, pp. 31-37.

----. (1992) 'The Syrian Private Industrial and Commercial Sectors and the State,' *International Journal of Middle East Studies,* v. 24, n. 2, May, pp. 207-230.

----. (1995), *The Political Economy of Syria under Asad*, London: I.B Taurus.

----. (2004), *Syria under Bashar al-Asad: Modernisation and the Limits of Change*. Adelphi Papers, London: Oxford University Press for IISS.

Poelling, Sylvia (1994) 'Investment Law No 10: Which Future for the Private Sector' in Eberhard Kienle, ed., *Contemporary Syria.*

Przeworski, Adam (2003), *States and Markets. A Primer in Political Economy*. Cambridge MA: Cambridge University Press.

Rodrigues, Francisco and Dani Rodrik, (1999), 'Trade Policy and Economic Growth: A Skeptic's Guide to the Cross-National Evidence,' *NBER Working Paper 7081,* April.

Rodrik, Dani (2002), 'Institutions Rule: The Primacy of Institutions over Geography and Integration in Economic Development.' Working Paper 9305. National Bureau of Economic Research, Cambridge, MA

Skocpol, Theda. (1979), *States and Social Revolution*. Cambridge: Cambridge University Press.

Stiglitz, Joseph E. (1989), 'The Economic Role of the State: Efficiency and Effectiveness.' in A. Heertje (ed.), *The Economic Role of the State,* London: Basil Blackwell and Bank Insinger de Beaucfort NV.

Sukkar, Nabil (1994) 'The Crisis of 1986 and Syria's Plan for Reform,' in Eberhard Kienle, ed., *Contemporary Syria,* London: British Academic Press, pp. 26-43.

Syrian Arab Republic (SAR), Central Bureau of Statistics, *Statistical Abstract*, various years.

Tilly, Charles (1990), *Coercion, Capital, and European States, AD 990-1990*. Cambridge, MA: Blackwell.

Trimberger, Ellen Kay. (1978), *Revolution from Above: Military Bureaucrats and Development in Japan, Turkey, Egypt and Peru*, New Brunswick, N.J.: Transaction Books.

Wade, Robert. (1990), *Governing the Market: Economic Theory and the Role of Government in East Asian Industrialization*, Princeton NJ: Princeton University Press.

Waldner, David. (1999), *State building and late development in Syria, Turkey, Korea and Taiwan,* Ithaca, N.Y : Cornell University Press.

Walton, John. (1984), *Reluctant Rebels: Comparative Studies of Revolution and Underdevelopment*. New York: Columbia University Press.

Weber, Max. (1964), *The Theory of Social and Economic Organization*. New York: Free Press.

Wilson, Rodney (1995), *Economic Development in the Middle East,* London: Routledge.

Yazigi, Jihad (2003), *Banking in Syria.* Paris: MEICA.

About the Authors

Søren Schmidt is a Project Researcher at the Danish Institute for International Studies, Copenhagen

Raymond Hinnebusch is Professor of International Relations and Middle East Politics at the University of St. Andrews, Scotland, and Director of the Centre for Syrian Studies.

The St Andrews Papers on Modern Syrian Studies is published by the Centre for Syrian Studies, University of St Andrews, Scotland and distributed by Lynne Rienner Publishers, Boulder, CO, USA. The series remit is to publish cutting edge contemporary research and analysis on modern Syria, with the focus on the contemporary economic "transition" (reform) and on Syria's current security problems.
http://www.st-andrews.ac.uk/~wwwir/syrian/

We invite submission of unsolicited papers, particularly papers that report on current empirical research on Syria. Send paper submissions to series editor, Raymond Hinnebusch, School of International Relations, University of St Andrews, St Andrews, Fife, Scotland, KY15 7SP, U.K. or by e-mail to rh10@st-andrews.ac.uk.